D0727678

POCKET STUDY SKILLS

Series Editor: **Kate Williams**, *Oxford Brookes University, UK*
Illustrations by Sallie Godwin

For the time-pushed student, the *Pocket Study Skills* pack a lot of advice into a little book. Each guide focuses on a single crucial aspect of study giving you step-by-step guidance, handy tips and clear advice on how to approach the important areas which will continually be at the core of your studies.

Published

14 Days to Exam Success
Blogs, Wikis, Podcasts and More
Brilliant Writing Tips for Students
Completing Your PhD
Doing Research
Getting Critical
Planning Your Essay
Planning Your PhD
Reading and Making Notes
Referencing and Understanding Plagiarism
Reflective Writing
Report Writing
Science Study Skills
Studying with Dyslexia
Success in Groupwork
Time Management
Writing for University

Pocket Study Skills
Series Standing Order
ISBN 978–0230–21605–1
(outside North America only)

You can receive future titles in this series as they are published by placing a standing order. Please contact your bookseller or, in case of difficulty, write to us at the address below with your name and address, the title of the series and the ISBN quoted above.

Customer Services Department, Macmillan Distribution Ltd, Houndmills, Basingstoke, Hampshire RG21 6XS, England

POCKET STUDY SKILLS

Jeanne Godfrey

WRITING FOR UNIVERSITY

palgrave
macmillan

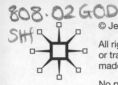

First published 2011 by
PALGRAVE MACMILLAN

Palgrave Macmillan in the UK is an imprint of Macmillan Publishers Limited, registered in England, company number 785998, of Houndmills, Basingstoke, Hampshire RG21 6XS.

Palgrave Macmillan in the US is a division of St Martin's Press LLC, 175 Fifth Avenue, New York, NY 10010.

Palgrave Macmillan is the global academic imprint of the above companies and has companies and representatives throughout the world.

Palgrave® and Macmillan® are registered trademarks in the United States, the United Kingdom, Europe and other countries

ISBN-13: 978-0-230-29120-1

This book is printed on paper suitable for recycling and made from fully managed and sustained forest sources. Logging, pulping and manufacturing processes are expected to conform to the environmental regulations of the country of origin.

A catalogue record for this book is available from the British Library.

10 9 8 7 6 5 4 3 2 1
20 19 18 17 16 15 14 13 12 11

Printed in China

Contents

Acknowledgements

My thanks go to my students for giving me the motivation to produce this guide and for the writing insights and experiences we have shared. I am grateful to Kate Williams for all her support and to Sallie Godwin for her wonderful illustrations that really bring this pocket guide to life. I would also like to thank Suzannah Burywood and Caroline Richards at Palgrave Macmillan for their professional and friendly approach to working with me on this book.

Finally I would like to thank Chris for his constant love and support.

Introduction

University study involves a significant amount of writing, no matter what subject you are doing. Writing also forms a key part of assessment at university, and tutors often require your written work to present a clear argument and to show other features of 'good academic writing'. However, because this type of writing is different in some ways from more everyday styles, what it actually consists of can seem a bit hidden and mysterious.

The aim of this book is to give you the language essentials for writing at university. This guide:

▶ gives you key words and phrases you need to use in academic writing

▶ uses real academic writing and a 'show not tell' approach to take you quickly and clearly through all the essential elements of successful academic writing: how to write critically; how to use sources; how to develop and emphasise your own writing voice; how to build your vocabulary; how to write clearly and how to edit and check your work

▶ shows you common student writing errors and how to avoid them

- gives you top tips and advice on the features and techniques you need to write successfully.

It's very important that you do develop the knowledge and ability to write clearly for your academic study, because writing provides the opportunity for you to really develop your thought processes, your understanding and your ideas, and is also an important way of communicating these things to your tutors. Regardless of how clever you are or how much you know, if you can't write it down clearly you won't get the marks!

Writing for University shows you what your tutors will expect from your writing and how to meet these expectations. It will help you to get the best marks possible for your work and make the best use of your talents, your tutors and your time. Writing for university study can actually be enjoyable, and this pocket guide will help you feel more confident about this key aspect of academic study.

Let's start to demystify things by looking at some common misconceptions about writing at university.

Myth versus fact

Myth	Fact
1 Writing well is a talent you either have or don't have.	Writing well is not a natural gift but something that needs to be *learnt and practised*. You may well struggle at first because the style and content of writing for university is new to you, but you will improve steadily and may even start to enjoy it.
2 There is one standard way of writing at university.	Many aspects of writing are common across subjects and assignment types, but you do also need to develop an awareness of the more specialised characteristics of your subject, task type and tutor's approach[1] (see Chapter 3).

[1] Throughout this book I use *discipline/subject*, *task/assignment* and *tutor/lecturer* interchangeably.

Myth	Fact
3 You need to find out all you can on the topic or title and put it all into your assignment.	Your tutor wants to see that you can discriminate between relevant and non-relevant sources[2] and be *selective* in what you include in your assignment (see Chapters 5 and 6).
4 Writing critically is when you say what is negative or incorrect about something.	In the academic world all knowledge, ideas and theories can be questioned and there is rarely an absolute answer. Being critical means using this questioning process to comment on and evaluate something. Your evaluation may be negative or positive or may simply highlight a different approach (see Chapters 5–7).
5 You should use lots of quotations.	The most highly valued way of using what you have read is to express and summarise it *in your own words*. You should only use quotations for very specific reasons (see Chapters 8 and 9).
6 Being original means coming up with a totally new idea or making a new discovery.	At undergraduate level you are not expected to make a unique contribution to knowledge, but to come to your own understanding of an issue. This unique understanding will arise naturally from how you decide to respond to your assignment title: your individual angle on it, which sources you select, how you use and evaluate them and the conclusions you come to (see all chapters).

[2] A *source* is anything you get information or ideas from: books, journal articles, websites, DVDs, lectures etc.

Myth	Fact
7 You shouldn't say what you think or use 'I' in assignments.	Using 'I' to say what your evaluations and conclusions are is increasingly acceptable. Your tutor *does* want to know what you think, as long as you have formed your view through analysis and evaluation of the evidence and other viewpoints (see Chapter 15).
8 You don't need to explain things your tutor already knows.	You do often need to be explicit in your writing so that your tutor can see that *you* have understood things. Your writing needs to be well structured and to explain things enough so that an educated and intelligent non-expert reader would be able to understand it (see Chapters 17 and 18).
9 Good writing[3] at university means writing in long sentences and using lots of long words.	Good writing is precise, clear and to the point. This means that you do need to use more formal vocabulary but not overly complex words or sentences (see Chapters 19 and 20).
10 Good writers think, then write, check and hand in.	Good writers make lots of mistakes and rewrite and correct their work many times before arriving at the final version (see Chapters 21–23).

[3] Writing at university is also called 'academic writing'.

Below is the third paragraph from an excellent second-year social science essay. The extract is annotated to show you the main features of academic writing.

Ageism is more disabling than ageing. Discuss.

Examples of clear communication to the reader

Examples of how the student has used sources

First sentence gives the link with the previous paragraph and also gives the topic of this one

Over the last 20 years research has shown that in addition to the reporting of conscious negative attitudes towards old people, there also seems to be an unconscious factor involved in ageism. Results from two studies conducted by Perdue and Gurtman in 1990 present evidence for the 'automaticity of ageism', namely that in a memory test, participants remembered more negative traits when the traits were linked to an old person than when linked to a younger one.

Referencing of source

Student's summary of a source in their own words

Words (*this/these*) that make the link from the previous sentence to this one

Repetitions of key words or similar words that help keep the paragraph on track

Clear sentence structure that is formal but not too long or complicated

Formal (but not overly so) words that are precise and therefore powerful

Importantly, these traits were not explicitly age-labelled; the participants were making the negative associations with older people on an unconscious or automatic level. The findings show that if the perceiver already has encoded negative associations, these can be unconsciously activated, thereby strengthening conscious negative attitudes and behaviours. In my view there are two minor flaws in the research. Firstly, Perdue and Gurtman report on associations rather than actual behaviour and should therefore perhaps talk about the automaticity of stereotyping rather than of ageism. Secondly, the assumption that negative associations with old people are unconsciously learnt at an early age has not yet been conclusively proven. Nevertheless, the evidence of unconscious negative associations with older people is important, not least because such associations may go unrecognised and be therefore harder to address and redress, increasing the disabling potential of ageism.

indicates that the student generally agrees with the source

Student's critical analysis and evaluation of the source

Student shows the relevance of the paragraph to the title

3 Understand your purpose and context

To produce a really successful piece of work you need to understand *why* you are writing and *what* you should be writing about. Key components of your writing context are your assignment title, the nature of your discipline, and your individual tutor's approach to the subject. Understanding your writing context will help you unlock and open the door to higher marks.

Understand what your subject wants

Different academic disciplines have different characteristics. Some disciplines, for example, will put more emphasis on measurable data (quantitative evidence) while others will give more weight to interpretative, subjective evidence (qualitative evidence). Getting a feel for the character of your subject is important, particularly if you are writing different assignments for different subjects.

Below is a table that gives examples of highly valued characteristics in different disciplines. You may like to use these very rough guidelines to help start you thinking and asking questions about what is highly valued by *your* tutors on *your* course.

Discipline	Common assignment types	Highly valued aspects and abilities
Biological science	Laboratory report	Detailed recording of methods and observations. Testable hypotheses. Completeness, thoroughness.
	Science literature review	Evaluation of relevant studies to show current controversies and changes in knowledge. Demonstration of where your study fits in.
History	Essay	Awareness of the different interpretations and debates on historical events.
	Document analysis	Interpretation and evaluation of primary documents and their implications. Rigorous recording of documentation.

Discipline	Common assignment types	Highly valued aspects and abilities
Law	Legal analysis essay	Finding relevant primary (e.g. legal statues) and secondary material. Clear understanding of all possible counter-arguments.
	Client letter	Application of relevant law to a specific client problem. Clarity and precision in advice given. Consistent use of terms, e.g. 'plaintiff'.
Psychological medicine	Written case report	Appreciation of patient's experience. Application of practical procedures to client's situation. Personal reflection on your approach and actions.
Computing	Client software design report	Design and/or application of software/programming to solve the client need.
Art and design	Written visual analysis	Personal and descriptive reactions supported by relevant theoretical concepts and ideas and examples.

Understand what your tutor wants

Different tutors may approach the same discipline from different directions and may also have slightly different ideas about what should go into a good piece of writing, so be proactive and ask your tutor what they consider to be most important and interesting about the subject.

Remember myth number 3 on page 2 – showing that you have *understood* the issue and that you can produce a well-structured argument is more important than just showing your tutor how much you know.

The assessment criteria for each written task will give you big clues as to what your tutor wants to see in your writing. Actually *reading* and *thinking about* the task criteria in your course or module handbook is time well spent. It's also important to remember that not all criteria are equal and that you should find out which ones your tutor values most.

Finally, assessment criteria can be written in quite complicated language so do ask your tutor if anything is unclear.

For more advice on assessment criteria, see Williams K (2009) *Getting Critical* p7–11 and Godwin J (2009) *Planning Your Essay* p3–8 in this series.

Understand your assignment title

If you have been given a title or specific brief to address, understanding it *fully* and *precisely* is the most important stage in producing a successful piece of writing. Your tutor wants to see that you have understood the *point* of the title and that you have identified underlying assumptions and issues.

- Give yourself plenty of time (preferably at least a week) to analyse and just think about the title before you start doing anything with it.

- Discuss it with other students and with your tutor.

- Note that shorter titles may look simpler but can in fact be more vague and therefore more difficult to interpret than longer ones.

- Try to read the title objectively rather than seeing what you want to see or expect to see.

Analyse your title

1 Underline and make sure you are on clear on:

C: words related to the **content** of the topic. If anything is ambiguous, ask your tutor for clarification (you may sometimes need to make your own decision on what something means).

F: the **function**/instruction words. Does the title ask you to analyse, compare (look at similarities and differences), contrast (focus on the differences) or some of these things together? Check the meaning of the function words (tip – if your title has *argue* or *discuss* in it, ask your tutor exactly what they want to see in the assignment).

S: the **scope** – what you are asked to cover and not cover, e.g. specific time periods or countries. If the scope is not explicit in the title (e.g. the title just says 'people') you will need to decide on the scope yourself and state this in your introduction.

2 Ask yourself as many questions as you can about the title:

Are any given facts accurate?
Are any cause–effect relationships implied and if so, can they be challenged?

Are there any underlying assumptions or value judgements?

Are there any hidden questions or issues?

What is the fundamental and most controversial point about the title?

Here is an example of a title analysis using the C, F and S categories.

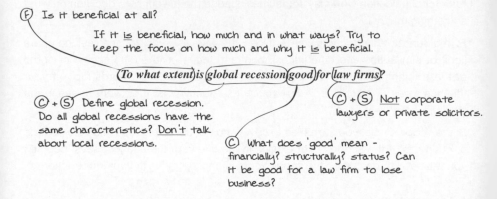

(F) Is it beneficial at all?

If it _is_ beneficial, how much and in what ways? Try to keep the focus on how much and why it _is_ beneficial.

(To what extent) is (global recession) (good) for (law firms)?

(C) + (S) Define global recession. Do all global recessions have the same characteristics? <u>Don't</u> talk about local recessions.

(C) What does 'good' mean - financially? structurally? status? Can it be good for a law firm to lose business?

(C) + (S) <u>Not</u> corporate lawyers or private solicitors.

For more advice on assignment titles, see Godwin J (2009) *Planning Your Essay* p23–7 and Williams K (2009) *Getting Critical* p44–8 in this series.

4 The five essential elements of writing

Imagine your finished piece of writing as a brightly shining star. At the centre of your star is your position on the assignment title that you have arrived at through the interactions between the five essential elements of academic writing.

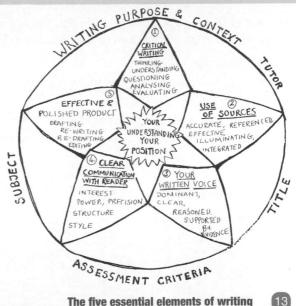

WRITING PURPOSE & CONTEXT

TUTOR

TITLE

ASSESSMENT CRITERIA

SUBJECT

① CRITICAL WRITING
THINKING
UNDERSTANDING
QUESTIONING
ANALYSING
EVALUATING

⑤ EFFECTIVE & POLISHED PRODUCT
DRAFTING
RE-WRITING
RE-DRAFTING
EDITING

YOUR UNDERSTANDING YOUR POSITION

② USE OF SOURCES
ACCURATE, REFERENCED
EFFECTIVE
ILLUMINATING,
INTEGRATED

④ CLEAR COMMUNICATION WITH READER
INTEREST
POWER, PRECISION
STRUCTURE
STYLE

③ YOUR WRITTEN VOICE
DOMINANT,
CLEAR,
REASONED,
SUPPORTED BY EVIDENCE

The precise nature and amount of each element needed will vary between different subjects and different writing tasks, but all five should be present in your writing. What will emerge at the centre of your star will be your own unique understanding of and response to the issue or question.

The rest of this book will take you through the five essential elements of academic writing shown in the star diagram on the previous page:

- writing critically
- using your sources correctly and effectively
- letting your own voice shine through
- communicating clearly with your reader
- producing a professional finished assignment via rewriting and editing.

Summary

- Tutors may differ in how they see the discipline and in what they regard as the most important assessment criteria. Be proactive and find out what your tutor feels is most important.

- Understanding your assessment criteria is important but try not to get obsessed by them – use them as a reminder of what you should be trying to do anyway. Also, remember to read your regulations. No matter how fantastic your assignment is, if you don't follow the deadline and submission regulations you may end up getting 0%.

- Don't make the mistake of reading your assignment title quickly, assuming you know what it means and then plunging into unfocused reading. Misunderstanding the assignment title is a common cause of low marks.

- The main purpose of any assignment is to act as a catalyst for learning, thinking and engaging with ideas and knowledge to arrive at your own understanding of your subject.

- The five essential elements of academic writing are fundamental to all assignment types.

5 What critical writing is

The fundamental purpose of any university course is to help you to develop the skill of critical thinking. The word *critical* as used in academic study does *not* mean:

▶ very important (e.g. to make a critical decision)
▶ very bad/dangerous (e.g. to be in a critical condition)
▶ to be negative/nasty about something (e.g. to criticise someone).

Being critical in academic work means looking at ideas, theories and evidence with a questioning attitude rather than taking them at face value. It means analysing things in detail, finding weaknesses *and* strengths and from your analysis deciding what *you* think and why.

At the start of your studies you may feel that it isn't right or possible to take a critical approach to the work of experts. However, you need to try and get over this feeling and accept that thinking with a critical approach is what you are at university to do. It is difficult work, and you will not be expected to have highly developed critical skills right from the start but to develop them over the time of your course.

Your tutors and assessment criteria will use phrases such as 'analyse the material and its implications', 'evaluate and synthesise', 'critically reflect' and 'show insight and independent thought'. These are all different stages in building a critical approach.

For more advice on critical thinking, see Williams K (2009) *Getting Critical* in this series.

One common reason for low marks is too much non-critical content (background information, description and explanation) and not enough critical content, particularly detailed analysis and evaluation. Below are some extracts from the student essay on ageism that show you the difference between non-critical and critical writing.

Non-critical writing: background or description

Gives the *what* or *how* of something but does not give reasons, comments or evaluation and does not try to persuade. It does not show your tutor that you have really understood the relevance and implications of the material.

For example …

> The causes of ageism were first suggested by Butler (1969); a lack of understanding of older people arising from a lack of interaction with them, combined with fears about becoming old and a consequent desire for distance. … Perdue and Gurtman (1990) found that in a memory test, participants remembered more negative traits when these were related to an old person.

Non-critical writing: explanation

Can *seem* more like critical writing because it gives reasons and perhaps a conclusion, but this is still just stating fact. An explanation does not evaluate, argue or try to persuade.

For example …

> Perdue and Gurtman concluded that unconscious negative associations were activated, thereby strengthening conscious negative attitudes and behaviours.

Critical writing: analysis

For example …

> Firstly, Perdue and Gurtman report on associations rather than actual behaviour and should therefore perhaps talk about the automaticity of stereotyping rather than of ageism. Secondly, the assumption that negative associations with old people are unconsciously learnt at an early age has not yet been conclusively proven.

Critical writing: evaluation

For example ...

> Neverthcless, the evidence of unconscious negative associations with older people is important, not least because such associations may go unrecognised and be therefore harder to address and redress, increasing the disabling potential of ageism.

Critical writing: argument

For example ...

> Because unconscious negative associations seem to be an important factor in ageism, we need to investigate further how they arise and raise people's awareness of them, if we are to reduce the degree of ageism in the UK.

A note on thinking and writing

Thinking and writing go hand in hand, and by writing you are developing and forming your thoughts. All writing (including scribbles, notes, written reflections, rough summaries and rough drafts) is an essential part of the thinking process. A lack of – or incorrect – analysis and evaluation in a finished piece of writing is often due to a lack of time (especially thinking time) spent on the task.

Below are the nine most common types of error students make when trying to write critically, with the problem and the solution to the error given after each set of examples.

1 Agreeing, disagreeing or giving a personal opinion

There are valid arguments both for and against stem cell research. I think that research on animals is vital.

I don't agree that ID cards will reduce identity theft.

Problem Agreement, disagreement and opinion are not critical evaluations but just your point of view unsupported by evidence. This is not acceptable in academic work.

Solution Forget your opinion; look at the arguments and evidence and *then* make up your mind. If the facts don't support your opinion, you're probably wrong. If the facts do support your opinion, show this by giving supporting evidence.

2 Starting by giving the answer which you then try to prove ('begging the question')

Ethical behaviour is not compatible with successful business practice. This essay will look at ...

| **Problem** You are assuming the answer before you have analysed the evidence. | **Solution** Give the evidence first and *then* evaluate whether/to what extent ethics and business are compatible. |

3 Writing about an opinion which you later give as a fact

Stem cell research is thought by some to be unethical. This essay will argue that the potential benefits of this type of research outweigh its unethical aspect.

| **Problem** In the first sentence you say that some people *think* stem cell research is unethical but in the second sentence you state as fact that stem cell research has an unethical aspect. | **Solution** If you want to argue that stem cell research is indeed unethical, you need to do so before you move on to look at potential benefits. |

4 Giving an empty, circular argument

The government should instigate an 'opt out' system of organ donation. This will ensure that a person's organs are automatically available for donation unless they have specified otherwise. Therefore, this legislation should be introduced as soon as possible.

| **Problem** There is no reasoning power here, just repetition. | **Solution** Explain *why* automatic donation is a good thing. |

5 Assuming causal connections or correlations

Children who play violent computer games commit more violent acts, therefore, the violence children see in computer games causes them to be violent.

Problem You are assuming a cause and effect link that may or may not exist. Other causes of increased violence could be the lack of physical activity when gaming or violent parents who incidentally tend to buy their children violent computer games.

Solution Look for evidence of other possible causes and then give *probable* correlations.

6 Making steps in reasoning that do not follow logically (a 'non-sequitur')

Identity theft is increasing, therefore the government should introduce identity cards.

Problem There is no explanation of how the use of identity cards relates to identity theft.

Solution Explain how and why identity cards would reduce the incidence of identity theft.

7 Being emotional, subjective or using 'empty persuaders'

Euthanasia is clearly immoral because it means killing people.

Problem The word *clearly* is used here to suggest the existence of evidence without actually giving any. Words such as *immoral* are subjective terms and meaningless without supporting evidence.

Solution Don't use words or phrases such as *there can be little doubt*, *obviously* and *surely* (they don't prove anything), and don't use words such as *clearly* unless directly related to evidence. Don't use subjective terms such as *immoral*, *outrageous*, *wonderful*.

8 Giving statements that do not analyse in enough detail

The growth in international trade requires improved legislation to control worldwide monopolies.

Problem The statement lumps all types of international trade together and so indicates a lack of detailed analysis.

Solution Do some detailed analysis and make distinctions between intra-industry, inter-industry, intra-firm and inter-firm trade.

9 Overgeneralising or making vague statements

Portable technology is used by everyone nowadays.

Men are stronger than women.

Some people think that euthanasia should be legal but the politicians disagree.

Problem These statements are too vague (which people and which politicians?) and so are very unlikely to be correct; things are rarely 'all or nothing'.

Solution Give a context that is as specific as possible, support your statement with evidence and use phrases that reflect the more complex reality, e.g. *the majority of/most/many/some/a minority of*.

Summary

- In the academic world all knowledge is open to question and debate.
- Writing critically means evaluating something and giving reasons for your evaluation.
- Think and write and write and think …
- Thinking and writing with a good critical eye is not a natural process and is hard work – if your brain hurts a bit you're doing it right.
- In academic work you don't have the right to make grand 'I think' statements without first doing the detailed analysis and evaluation.
- The difference between an average assignment and an excellent one is the quality of the critical evaluation it contains and the clarity of the links made between the evidence and the student's own ideas.

Essential element 2: Use your sources correctly and effectively

There are two ways of using sources in your academic writing:

▶ using the *exact* words of the source = quotation
▶ putting the source information/ideas into your own words = paraphrase or summary.

Whenever you are about to quote or paraphrase a source in your writing, ask yourself:

Why do I want to use this source?

How does it relate to the assignment title?

How does it relate to my argument?

Have I analysed and evaluated it?

What am I going to *say* about it?

Quotations are *exact* phrases or sentences taken from your sources. Here is an example of a short quotation from a student essay on business ethics:

> A second, even stronger argument for the view that businesses should be ethical is that '… good ethics is synonymous with good management' (Collins 1994 p2).

Only use quotations for special occasions

Only quote if you feel that you have found a particularly powerful phrase. The number of quotations you use will vary according to your discipline and assignment type – you may use quite a few if you are writing a literature essay but not use any if you are writing a lab report. As a very general rule, only use short quotations once or twice a page at most.

You can use quotations to:

☑ state a fact or idea which the author has expressed in a unique and powerful way

- ✅ establish or summarise an author's argument or position
- ✅ provide an interesting/important start or end to your essay
- ✅ give the reader an original extract you are going to discuss in detail (usually longer quotations).

Don't use quotations because:

- ❌ you think that putting them in will impress your tutor
- ❌ you haven't given enough time to reading critically and taking notes so it seems much easier to cut and paste quotations into your assignment rather than putting the ideas into your own words.

Quotations: the essentials

1 Introduce them correctly

To introduce a quotation, either use the author's family name as the subject of your sentence, so not in brackets, or keep the author's name out of your sentence and put it in brackets after the quotation.

Examples:

> Benjamin (1970) argues that '… no translation would be possible if in its ultimate essence it strove for likeness of the original' (p41).

or

A second, even stronger argument for the view that businesses should be ethical is that '… good ethics is synonymous with good management' (Collins 1994 p2).

2 Use the correct punctuation

Use a *colon* if you use a complete sentence to introduce the quotation.

Example:

Winterson uses the sea as a metaphor for life: 'Shoals of babies vied for life' (Winterson 2005 p3).

Use a *comma* if you use an introductory phrase with the quotation.

Examples:

As Tomalin (2010) states, 'Pepys was … mapping a recognizably modern world' (p148).

According to Brandon (2008), 'History is a record of relationships' (p151).

Don't use any punctuation if you integrate your quotation smoothly into the rest of your sentence.

Examples:

Polkinghorne describes a quantum as 'a kind of little bullet' (Polkinghorne 2002 p10).

One of Oswald's most important findings is that 'joblessness is a major source of distress' (Oswald 1997 p1825).

3 Don't change anything

Don't make *any* changes to the punctuation or wording of the actual quotation.

- If you need to show that the quotation is not the start of a sentence, use '...
- Don't change the first letter in the quotation from lower case to upper case. If you don't quote to the end of a sentence, again use ...' Don't give it a full-stop that wasn't there in the original.
- If you want to leave anything out in the middle of a quotation use ...
- If you need to add anything to make the quotation clearer to the reader, use [ ] to show what you have added.
- If your quotation already has a quotation within it, show this by giving it the alternate type of quotation marks to the ones you use for the main quotation (e.g. double quotes within single).

Let's look at an example of using a quotation that demonstrates all of the above.

Source extract:

> This use of percentage GDA signals on front-of-pack labeling has been promoted by some sections of the food industry as an alternative to a 'traffic-light' signposting system recommended by the Food Standards Agency (FSA).
>
> Lobstein T, Landon J and Lincoln P (2007) *Misconceptions and misinformation: The problems with Guideline Daily Amounts (GDAs)* National Heart Forum report

Student quotation:

> Lobstein et al (2007) state that ' … use of percentage GDA [Guideline Daily Amounts] signals … has been promoted … as an alternative to a "traffic light" signposting system …' (p1).

4 Show that it *is* a quotation

For short quotations (up to two lines) you must use quotation marks. You can use either single ' ' or double " " quotation marks (ask your tutor which they prefer) but be consistent.

For longer quotations don't use quotation marks. Instead, use a colon and indentation.

Example:

> In law, where there is no *active* termination of life, it may not be unlawful killing:
>> … the law draws a crucial distinction between cases in which a doctor decides not to provide, or to continue to provide, for his patient treatment or care which could or might prolong his life, and those in which he decides actively to bring his patient's life to an end.[3]
>
> This distinction, however, does not provide a legal solution in cases where …

5 Check that your quotation is directly relevant to your point and always comment on your quotation

Use your analysis and evaluation of your source to *comment* on it – to tell your reader what significance it has for your argument.

Extract from student essay:

> A second, even stronger argument for the view that good ethics in business do exist is: '… good ethics is synonymous with good management' (Collins 1994 p2). Collins's view is borne out by examples of businesses that are successful in part because they focus on the human element of management, such as …

This sentence introduces the quotation and shows how the student is using it to support her own point.

The student is about to give concrete examples as further support for her own point that businesses can be ethical.

What went wrong here?

❌ Grosjean (1984) believes that 'bilinguals range from being very poor to being very competent translators' (p257).

The problem? Not a special/powerful idea and so not worth quoting – the student should have used their own words.

❌ Logan (1999) states that 'The second world war ended in 1945' (p111).

The problem? You don't usually need to quote common knowledge.

❌ The main benefit of organ transplant is that it saves lives. As stated by Smith (2005), 'heart transplantation can save lives, but the procedure carries serious risks and complications and a high mortality rate' (p12).

The problem? The second part of the quotation contradicts the student's point.

❌ Hairshine.com conducted a survey on the product. The survey showed that '82.7% of the interviewees were satisfied with the product and 10% were not satisfied' (Marchant 2010 p20). Customer satisfaction should be a priority for all companies …

The problem? The statistics are not special enough to quote. Another problem is that the student does not comment on or evaluate them.

✗ Using animal organs for transplantation is beneficial, as patients are not forced to wait as long for transplants. As stated by Kline (2005), 'advances in genetic techniques mean that there is less chance of animal organs being rejected by the human immune system' (p53).

The problem? The quotation does not relate to the student's point about reduced waiting lists.

9 Using your words – paraphrase and summary

When using sources you should use your own words and writing style as much as possible. Re-expressing sources in this way is at the heart of academic writing but it is a difficult skill that takes practice.

Using your own words to restate source material will enable you to:

- find out for *yourself* whether or not you really understand your material
- show your *tutor* that you have understood it
- restate information/ideas more clearly and simply
- restate the information/ideas in a way that supports your own argument
- express the information/ideas in your own style so that they fit smoothly into the rest of your assignment
- show your tutor that you have been able to pick out the main message of a text (summarising)
- show that you understand the position of key authors on a topic and how they relate to each other (summarising).

Paraphrasing

You will sometimes want to re-express a single idea and/or just one or two sentences from a source. This is referred to as paraphrasing.

Here is an example. Note that the student introduces their paraphrase to support their own point.

Source extract:

> It is clearly best if the [stem] cells used in transplantation can be taken from the patient him- or herself, to avoid rejection by the body. While embryonic cells have been proposed as a means of avoiding rejection problems, even early embryonic cells have surface molecules which can cause an immune response.
>
> Jones D (2002) *A Submission to The House of Lords Select Committee on Stem Cell Research.* London: The Linacre Centre for Healthcare Ethics.

Student paraphrase:

> Another key reason for moving research away from use of embryonic cells is that of tissue rejection. Jones (2002) points out that this can occur even with embryonic cells and that it is therefore better to use the patient's own cells in transplantation (p3).

Summarising

A much more common reason for using your own words and style is to summarise a whole section, chapter, article or book.

Examples:

Student summary of one article:

> Oswald (1997) argues that economic performance does have an effect on personal happiness, but that the degree of happiness depends more on whether or not you have a job than on how much or little you earn.

Student summary of the position of three different sources (two books and one article):

> Opponents of the concept of ethics in business include those who claim that making a profit is the only responsibility a business has to society (Freidman 1970 cited in Fisher and Lovell 2003). Wolf (2008) shares this view and Prindl and Prodham (1994) suggest that business finance is a 'value-neutral' activity that does not need to consider social consequences.

Steps for writing a good paraphrase or summary

1 Read, re-read and make notes until you really understand your material.*

2 Reflect on the material and ask yourself what you would say if a friend asked you what it was about.

3 Use some of your own words and phrases in your notes. Your notes should also record which phrases are copied down word for word (quotations), which are a mix of you and the source, and which are your comments and ideas.

4 Write your paraphrase or summary from your memory and notes rather than by looking back at the original text.

5 Check that your paraphrase or summary directly supports your point.

* For more advice on making notes see
Godfrey J (2010) *Reading and Making Notes*,
Williams K (2009) *Getting Critical* p30–1 and
Williams K and Carroll J (2009) *Referencing
and Understanding Plagiarism* in this series.

How much do you need to change the original text?

This is really the wrong question. If you follow the steps on p39 you shouldn't need to ask yourself whether you have made enough changes from the original. However in our 'cut and paste' culture it may be necessary to check this sometimes. A short answer to this question is that you need to change nearly everything and to fully rewrite the source information – there is no such thing as a 'half and half' approach in academic work.

To show you what I mean, below are three student paraphrases of the Jones text extract. The first two paraphrases have not been properly rewritten and would count as plagiarism. Only the last paraphrase is good enough and I have annotated it to show you some grammatical, vocabulary and structural techniques you can use to rewrite source information.

Source extract:

> It is clearly best if the [stem] cells used in transplantation can be taken from the
> patient him- or herself, to avoid rejection by the body. While embryonic cells have been
> proposed as a means of avoiding rejection problems, even early embryonic cells have
> surface molecules which can cause an immune response.
> Jones, D (2002) *A Submission to The House of Lords Select Committee on Stem Cell
> Research.* The Linacre Centre for Healthcare Ethics.

Student paraphrase 1: ✗

The order of information, sentence pattern and about half the text is unchanged (underlined)

Another key reason for moving research away from use of embryonic cells is that of tissue rejection. It is best if the cells used for transplants are taken from the patient to avoid rejection by the body. Cells from embryos have been proposed as a means of avoiding problems of rejection, but even early embryonic cells have molecules on the surface that can cause a rejection response.

Student paraphrase 2: ✗

Another key reason for moving research away from use of embryonic cells is that of tissue rejection. Jones (2002) points out that tissue used for transplanting can be taken from patients so that rejection does not occur. Cells from embryos have been proposed as a means of avoiding rejection problems, but even these cells have surface molecules that can create a response from the immune system.

Still too many phrases from the original and this paraphrase still has exactly the same information and sentence pattern as the original text.

Student paraphrase 3: ✔

First sentence helps paraphrase flow smoothly into the essay and shows how it will support the student's own point.

Student's own words and style. All words changed except for 'embryonic cells', 'rejection' and 'molecular'.

> Another key reason for moving research away from use of embryonic cells is that of tissue rejection. Jones (2002) points out that rejection problems do occur with cells taken from embryos due to the molecules on the cell surface, and that it is therefore better to use the patient's own cells for transplantation procedures.

Tips for rewriting the original
- Reverse the order of information
- Use different sentence structures
- Use synonyms, e.g. immune response → rejection problem
- Use different word forms e.g. embryonic cells → cells from embryos.

Other things to watch out for when paraphrasing or summarising

▶ Not giving your paraphrase a reference. Although you are using your own words, the idea/information is from your source so you must always reference.

▶ Accidently changing the meaning – the way to avoid this is to try to make sure that you understand accurately what you have read.

▶ In a summary, keeping in too much detail. A short summary may only be one or two sentences long and even the most detailed summary should never be longer than one third of the original.

▶ Doing too much paraphrasing. Continually paraphrasing short sections from sources is almost as bad as quoting every few lines. Try to emphasise *your* argument more, summarise sources more and show how they relate to each other and to your argument. Only paraphrase short sections of text to focus on essential points.

▶ Adding your own comments within the paraphrase or summary – keep these to before or after it.

▶ Not showing clearly where your paraphrase or summary begins and end (see the next section).

Remember to comment on your paraphrase or summary: Just as with quotations, there is no point in paraphrasing or summarising a source if you do not evaluate it and show its relevance to your point (see Chapter 13, p60).

All referencing styles fall into one of two categories.

1 **Author/year system:** author's surname and year of publication in the body of the assignment and a detailed list in alphabetical order of author surname at the end.

Example (Harvard referencing style)

In your work	In your references
Collins (1994 p2) states that 'good ethics is synonymous with good management'.	Collins J W (1994). Is business ethics an oxymoron? *Business Horizons* Volume 37, Issue 5 pp1-8.

or

2 **Numeric/footnote system:** a sequence of numbers in the body of the assignment and a numbered list of references at the end of each page or of the whole assignment.

Example (Numeric style British Standard)

In your work	In your references
Collins (1) states that managing a business well requires an ethical approach.	1. Collins, J W. Is business ethics an oxymoron? *Business Horizons*, 37 (5), 1994.

Your course may have its own variation of a particular referencing style so always check this with your tutor or course handbook.

For more advice on referencing styles, see Williams K and Carroll J (2009) *Referencing and Understanding Plagiarism* in this series.

Using referencing to emphasise different aspects of your source

1 Emphasising the information

If you want to emphasise the *information* in your source rather than the author, give the in-text reference at the end of the sentence in brackets (or as a number if you are using numeric referencing).

> Although the law overlaps with ethics, it usually only regulates the lowest level of acceptable behaviour (Crane and Matten 2007).

2 Emphasising both the information and the author

To emphasise the information and the author equally, refer in a general way to the fact that research or other work has been done but again only give the specific reference at the end of the sentence in brackets. This technique is useful for bringing together similar research or work and for referencing several authors together. Note that for this type of general reporting, the verb is usually used in the present perfect tense ('… has indicated').

Research has indicated that job satisfaction is linked to regulating emotion (Cote and Morgan 2002, Barrick 2002).

You can also use the passive tense ('… has been suggested'). This also emphasises both the information and the authors.

It has been suggested that violent films have a negative effect on children's behaviour (Carlton 1999, Cyprian 2001).

3 Emphasising the author

If you want to emphasise the specific author/s of the source, give the author *as part of your sentence*, with only the year of publication in brackets (or use a number at the end of the sentence). You can also use this method when you want to show that you have reviewed the literature and that you know who the key authors are and which of them hold similar views to each other.

Wolf (2008) shares this view and Prindl and Prodham (1994) also suggest that …

What went wrong here?

Sentence from student essay	Problem
According to (Reynolds, 2000) there is no strong evidence of long-term damage to health.	*Reynolds* is part of the sentence so should not be in brackets.
According to Padash 2000 there is no strong evidence of long-term damage to health.	*2000* should be in brackets.
George Marchais (1984) discusses three main factors.	Don't use the author's first name – just their family name.
A strong economy relies on moderate taxation methods (Sloman, *Economics* 3rd Edition).	Don't include details such as the title or edition within your assignment – save these for the bibliography or 'references' section.
Smoking and related illnesses cause over 500,000 deaths annually in the UK.	There is no reference at all for this information.

11 How to avoid accidental plagiarism

Below is an eight-point summary of what to remember and what to do in order to avoid plagiarising accidently in your writing.

1 Remember the two default rules

Rule 1: *No reference = your own words* and *your own ideas*

A sentence that doesn't have a reference is assumed to be *all* you – your own ideas, words and style. Therefore an unreferenced paraphrase or summary is plagiarism.

Rule 2: *No quotation marks/indentation = your own words*

Something with a reference but no quotation marks/indentation is assumed to be your own words. Therefore if you use a quotation and reference but don't also use quotation marks/indentation, it might be considered as plagiarism because you are implying that you have used your own words.

2 It's all or nothing when using sources

When using a source you must either change just about *everything* (except key terms) or change *nothing* and use it as a quotation. A 'half and half' approach is not acceptable in academic work.

3 An assignment that has too much quotation, paraphrase and summary is a form of plagiarism

You can't really claim that *you* wrote an assignment if 80% of it is quotation, paraphrase or summary of other people's work.

4 Putting a source into your own words is good, but not giving it a reference is bad

You should paraphrase and summarise rather than quote but *the information* in your paraphrase still comes from someone else – so reference it!

5 One reference is often not enough

Putting one reference at the end of a paragraph that is a mix of you and sources is not enough; you must make clear where every switch is between you and your sources. This means that many of your sentences will need either a reference or a reference reminder phrase.

Example: *first/main reference*

(Dickinson (2009)) argues that the language translation industry, for example translation brochures and websites, is the key to helping Britain recover from recession. (He also stresses) the importance of hiring professional translators.

Reference reminder phrase

6 Websites should be treated in the same way as paper sources

Anything from any type of website (including Wikipedia) needs to be referenced in the body of your assignment in the same way (author/year or number) as any other type of source.

7 Don't give the impression that you have read something when you haven't

If you read something by author X that mentions author Y, make it clear in your reference which source you actually read by using the phrase *cited in* or *in*.

In the example below the student makes it clear that he has read Fisher and Lovell *not* Freidman.

> Opponents of the concept of ethics in business include those who claim that making a profit is the only responsibility a business has to society (Freidman 1970 cited in Fisher and Lovell 2003).

8 A list of sources is not enough

Having a detailed list of sources at the end of your assignment but no references within the assignment is still plagiarism – how can your reader tell which ideas in the assignment are yours and which aren't?

You must reference *both* in the body of your work (see pp44 and 45) *and* then again in your list of list of sources/bibliography.

For more advice on using sources and referencing, see Godfrey J (2009) *How to Use Your Reading in Your Essays* and Williams K and Carroll J (2009) *Referencing and Understanding Plagiarism*.

Summary

- Being able to use your sources accurately and effectively starts at the reading and note-making stage.

- Be clear about *why* you want to use a source.

- Save quotations for special occasions.

- Use your own words to give powerful comparisons and summaries of sources.

- Use a source to support a point you make, not as a substitute for making it.

- Avoid accidental plagiarism by remembering the writing default rules and keeping a careful track of exactly where you got your information from.

- You will only get credit for your ideas if your tutor can distinguish them clearly from those of your sources, so use referencing and reference reminder phrases.

Essential element 3:
Let your own voice shine through

12   Show the voices of your sources

In order to let your own voice shine through in your assignment you also need to show your tutor the other voices (your sources). You do this by accurate and referenced quotations, paraphrases and summaries (see previous chapter), and also by using appropriate verbs, often called reporting verbs.

Use the right verb for the job

Reporting verbs show that you understand exactly what an author is doing in the original text, so you need to use the right verb.

    Lawton (2009) <u>describes</u> the different uses of pain relieving drugs.

is very different from

    Lawton (2009) <u>questions</u> the different uses of pain relieving drugs.

To help you choose the right verb, ask yourself what the author is trying to *do* in different parts of their text – are they explaining, describing, arguing or doing something else? Even more importantly, what are they trying to do *overall*: arguing against a different point of view? Giving recommendations? Reporting findings and their implications?

Common reporting verbs

argue	identify
address	investigate
challenge	list
conclude	point out
conduct	propose
define	provide
demonstrate	question
deny	reject
describe	show
discuss	state
examine	suggest
explain	trace
highlight	

Use the right grammar for the verb

In the active tense all reporting verbs need to use one of three structures:

Structure	Example ✔
verb + noun	Research *shows* a link between folklore and history.
verb + that + independent clause	Cote and Morgan *proposed* that job satisfaction is linked to regulating emotion.
verb + what/why/where/who/whether + independent clause	Lin and Moon *show* why the public is very interested in medical stories.

Some reporting verbs (e.g. *show*) can be followed by all three structures, depending on what you are using them for, but most verbs use only one or two structures. Try to notice how these verbs are used as you read and check the correct grammatical structures if you are unsure.

What went wrong here?

Sentence from student essay	Problem
According to me, the issue of global warming is …	*According to* is only used to report other authors.
Kerlinger (1969) quotes that 'Science is a misused and misunderstood word' (p1127).	The verb *quote* is only used to say that one author has quoted another author.
As Collins (1994) cites, 'good ethics is synonymous with good management' (p2).	As with *to quote*, we only use *cite* when author X cites author Y.
Researchers in the UK are undergoing studies about the possible effects of the drug.	*Undergo* is only used for the people or things to which the experiment or treatment is done. The sentence should be either *… conducting studies on the possible effects …* or *… studying/examining/investigating the possible effects …*
To summarise Karlov's argument, he mentions that playing chess uses a similar part of the brain as playing music.	*Mention* is only used to report a minor point, and so is not the right verb for introducing a summary.

Sentence from student essay	Problem
Lupton discusses about the portrayal of medicine and health in the media.	A common mistake that really annoys tutors! *Discuss, describe, define, study, examine* are **not** followed by *about, in, at* or *on*. The sentence should be *Lupton discusses the portrayal ...*
This essay will argue a link between regulating emotions and job satisfaction.	Right verb but wrong grammatical structure – *argue* needs verb + *that* + independent clause. *This essay will argue that there is a link between ...*
As implied by Murtaz (2007), 'patient care should be the primary motive for developments in the NHS' (p1).	Murtaz's statement is explicit, not something which he has only implied but not openly said. The student should have used a verb such as *state, argue* or *assert* rather than *implied*.
The idea of using a computer program to collectively edit a website was perceived by Cunningham and Beck in the late 1990s.	The verb should be *conceived*, meaning when an idea is first thought of. *Perceived* means 'thought of/viewed in a particular way'.
The ideas portrayed in the report are not new.	The student meant *conveyed*, meaning 'communicated'. *Portrayed* means to represent or describe in a particular way.

13 Show your *own* voice

The voice your tutor most wants to see in your assignment is yours; they want to know what *you* consider to be important and why. Your written voice will emerge through:

▶ the sources you choose and how you interpret and use them

▶ your evaluation of sources and how you link them to *your* points.

▶ the clarity of the referencing you use to show which ideas are yours and which aren't

▶ the soundness, clarity and structure of your argument and assignment

Showing your evaluation of sources

Your evaluations are the clearest way of making your voice shine, and a common reason for low marks is not making clear links between the ideas from your sources and your *own* position.

Below are two versions of an essay extract. In version A, the student cites Baber but does not evaluate this source or link it to his own ideas – he just goes straight on to his next source. In version B, the student shows how Baber's findings are relevant to his own argument (and by doing so also shows *why* he will cite Bulmer and Patel).

Version A ✗	Version B ✓
Baber (2006) demonstrates that corporations using portable devices should ensure their administrators have a background in computer and network security. Both Bulmer (2007) and Patel (2009) demonstrate that staff training programmes …	Baber (2006) demonstrates that corporations using portable devices should ensure their administrators have a background in computer and network security (p3). I would argue that this is crucial but that it is probably even more essential to have *ongoing* staff training as part of an organised educational and training approach. Indeed, both Bulmer (2007) and Patel (2009) show that staff training programmes …

An example of student written voice

Below is version B of the extract again, annotated this time to show you how the
student has let their written voice shine through. Chapters 14–16 will show you how
to use the specific aspects of language highlighted.

Baber (2006) demonstrates that corporations
using portable devices should ensure their
administrators have a background in computer
and network security.

I would argue that this is crucial, but that
it is probably even more essential to have
ongoing staff training as part of an organised
educational and training approach.

Indeed, both Bulmer (2007) and Patel (2009)
show that staff training programmes …

Positive evaluative verb to report
Baber.

Good choice of a main expert
source and correct and concise
summary of what they say.

Clear indication of how Baber is
relevant to student's argument.

Clearly shows student's evaluation
and own position.

Shows a high degree of certainty
(but not absolute)

Shows that student understands
how other key sources relate to
their point.

14 Your voice: verbs

Using reporting verbs to show what you think about a source

I have looked at using verbs to show that you understand what an author is doing in their text. Another important and powerful use of reporting verbs is for showing *your* evaluation of what the author does.

Read the sentence below from an article by Deborah Lupton:

'Research would certainly suggest that the lay public has a strong interest in health and medical issues in the media.'

If you shared Lupton's view and wanted to show this in your assignment, you would use a positive verb (e.g. *show*) to introduce what she says and then go on to agree with her explicitly:

Lupton (1998) <u>shows that</u> people are very interested in stories and news about medical and health matters. Indeed, some of the most popular current TV shows are hospital dramas.

However, if your argument was that the public does *not* have an interest in health and medicine in the media, you would need to use a less positive verb (e.g. *assert*). These verbs are not negative in themselves, but they do leave the door open for you to then disagree with the author:

> Lupton (1998) <u>asserts that</u> people are very interested in stories and news about medical and health matters. However, a large amount of media coverage given to such issues does not necessarily demonstrate that we are really interested in them.

Positive verbs	Neutral verbs	Less positive verbs
confirm	argue	assert
demonstrate	conclude	assume
establish	describe	claim
find	discuss	contend
illustrate	examine	maintain
note	explain	
observe	give	
point out	state	
show	suggest	

What went wrong here?

Sentence from student essay	Problem
Laurent (2007) claims that 'genetic engineering is the most important advance in medicine since the development of vaccines' (p15). This essay will demonstrate that this is clearly the case.	*Claim* is usually used as a negative verb, but the student goes on to agree with Laurent. A positive or neutral verb should have been used.
Tanen (2000) established that visual imprinting occurs in infancy. However, this was shown to be incorrect by later studies.	*Established* is a very positive verb but the student goes on to say that Tanen was wrong.

Other language to show your position towards a source

Positive phrases	Negative phrases
Smith's research ...	Smith's research ...
benefits from	fails to consider
considers all aspects	neglects the fact that
correctly identifies	overlooks
examines in great detail	suffers from
	wrongly assumes
Smith's research is ...	Smith's research is ...
conclusive	flawed
important	inconclusive
interesting	limited
reliable	questionable
sound	unreliable
valid	unsatisfactory

Using 'I'

Using 'I' is increasingly acceptable and even encouraged because it is a clear way of showing your tutor your position and voice. The important thing about using 'I' is not to fall into the trap of using it to give your personal opinions or to write in a chatty style. Remember that you have to earn the right to use 'I' by analysing and evaluating your sources (unless you are writing a reflective assignment) and then using 'I' to give your informed and supported viewpoint.

When to use 'I'	Examples ✔
When you want to state what you will do or have done.	*I will attempt to show that …* *I will examine/argue/suggest/propose …* *I have demonstrated that …*
To evaluate a source or to state/clarify your position.	*I would suggest that these findings are important and would add that …*
When your assignment requires reflective writing.	*I think that the experiment would have been better if …*

When *not* to use 'I'	Examples ✗
To give a personal opinion that is not supported (or worse contradicted!) by the evidence.	*I feel discouraged by the current state of the environment.* *I think that we should all work until at least 65.* *I don't like animal testing because …* *The study indicates that homeopathy is not effective but I still feel that it works.* *I believe in the power of the mind.* *I prefer towns to cities.*
To describe methodology, stages and processes where it is not important who did what. Instead, use the passive tense: *The equipment was washed in saline solution.*	*I washed the equipment in saline solution.*
To give information or to state a fact. Instead just give the fact: *Dickens was born in 1812*	*I read that Dickens was born in 1812.*

Note – you can use *think* or *feel* if you are careful (e.g. *I feel that Pulu's research is flawed because …*) but this might give the impression that you have not used an analytical thought process; it's usually better to use *I suggest/argue* or *My view is that …*

Using 'we'

Students sometimes overuse *we* because they are trying not to use 'I' or because they are trying to be formal. There are four common uses of 'we' but only one of them is appropriate for formal writing.

When to use 'we'	Example ✔
To indicate collaborative/team work	*We each interviewed 10 students*

When not to use 'we'	Examples ✗
'We' meaning 'I' This can be ambiguous (do you mean just you or a team?) and also sounds archaic and overly formal – it's much better to use 'I'.	*We will propose in this essay that* … *In this essay we argue that …*
To refer to both you and the reader This use of 'we' is ambiguous (do you really mean just you, you and the reader, or a team?) and sounds as if you are telling the reader what to think. Instead use: *It should be noted that …* *Table 5 shows that …* *The data suggest a link …* *I suggest that the data show a link …*	*We should note that …* *We also need to consider the possibility of …* *We can see from Table 5 that …* *We can conclude from the data that there is a link …*

When not to use 'we'	Examples ✗
To refer to society/everyone You can use 'we' to state a known fact, but it might sound presumptuous (does everybody know?). Never use *we all …* It's much better to just give the fact (*Smoking is addictive*) or to use the passive tense (*The addictive nature of smoking is well established*).	*We know that smoking is addictive.* *We all know that smoking is addictive.*
'We' can also be too informal and personal. It's better to write *Large-scale deforestation causes …*	*When we cut down forests, we cause …*
'We' often goes hand in hand with an over-generalisation – not acceptable in academic writing (see p25).	*We should decriminalize all drugs.* *We all want to live in a fairer society.*
Spoken/presentation style phrases These types of 'we' phrases are fine for spoken presentations (you might hear your tutor use them in a lecture) but they are too informal for writing.	*We will begin by …* *We are going to discuss …* *We would like to point out that …* *We shall now move on to …*

Be wary of giving statements or conclusions of absolutely certainty such as:

❌ *The data <u>prove</u> the existence of automatic ageism.*
❌ *Removing speed cameras <u>will result in</u> an increase in the number of road deaths.*
❌ *Children are <u>definitely</u> more politically aware than in previous generations.*

Even though you think there is overwhelming evidence for something, someone else may think differently and even the most eminent scientists have to accept that they might be wrong (even if secretly they think they have found 'the answer').

We show this contestable nature of knowledge by using 'cautious' language such as 'I suggest'; 'this might indicate'; 'this indicates a tendency'; 'it is probably the case that'. Don't be fooled by textbooks that imply certainty for teaching purposes. Instead, have a look at an academic journal article in your subject area and note how many times the author uses phrases to water down the certainty of their claim. An additional benefit of using cautious language is that it helps persuade your reader rather than sounding as if you are telling them what to think.

Below are phrases ordered according to their certainty level. Use them in your own writing to develop a voice that acknowledges different degrees of certainty and the contestable nature of knowledge.

Verb phrases

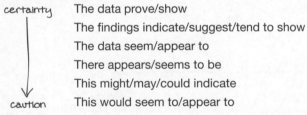

certainty

The data prove/show

The findings indicate/suggest/tend to show

The data seem/appear to

There appears/seems to be

This might/may/could indicate

caution

This would seem to/appear to

Adverb/verb phrases

certainty   This strongly/certainly/definitely suggests

                 This almost certainly/definitely suggests/shows/indicates

                 I would strongly suggest

caution   This perhaps suggests

Adjective/noun phrases

certainty   This proves with absolute certainty

                 It is almost certainly/It is highly probable

                 There is a good/strong/definite possibility

                 It is probable/likely

                 There is a tendency for

                 It is possible

caution   There is a slight/small possibility

NB: Some tutors don't like the use of verbs such as *suggests* for inanimate objects (e.g. *The data suggest that ...*) so check this with your tutor.

Summary

- You can only develop a clear voice through good-quality thinking and engagement with your subject and assignment task.
- You need to show all the voices in your assignment but *yours* is the one that should stand out.
- Don't write like a textbook – your tutor wants to see that you appreciate the contestable nature of knowledge.
- Ensure that your written voice is clear, precise and shows the appropriate degrees of certainty through good use of reporting verbs, *I/we* and cautious language.

Essential element 4: Write for your reader

The outward success of any piece of work is judged by the audience – in this case your tutor. You want to avoid your tutor having to ask themselves lots of questions when they are marking your work about what you mean or about whether one point connects to the other. A successful piece of writing has good-quality content, a clear structure and a direct, precise style.

Write for your reader 75

You need to structure your writing clearly to allow your ideas to shine. The exact way you structure your writing will depend on your particular writing context (a lab report will have a different structure to a discursive essay). However, all written pieces should have the basic structural ingredients outlined here.

INTRODUCTION – say what you are going to do

Interpret the issue and say why is it important.

Interpret and define key terms.

Say how you will answer the issue/question and the order in which you will do so.

BODY – do what you said you would do

Start to explore the issue.

Continue to explore and develop the issue.

Push further and identify extra dimensions and distinctions within the issue.

Move on to clarify what you feel is at the heart of the position you have arrived at.

CONCLUSION – say what you have done

Bring things together by summarising what you have said and clarifying the position you have arrived at.

Importantly, the three main sections of your piece should connect logically and should match up.

Always do a detailed plan before you start writing out in full – if you don't, it's very easy to end up with an assignment that is a bundle of mismatched pieces. For example, if you were writing the essay '*Ageism is more disabling than ageing. Discuss*' and you spent most of the essay body giving evidence for how ageism is *not* a serious problem, it would then be odd to state in your conclusion that ageism is a significant problem and very much more disabling than natural aging.

For more advice on essay planning and structure, see Godwin J (2009) *Planning Your Essay* in this series.

Introduction

Body

Conclusion

Avoid doing this!

Use signposting language

A useful way of bringing out the structure of your assignment is to give your reader language 'signposts'. Don't use them just for the sake of it but do use them to tell your reader where you are going in your writing.

Useful signpost phrases

Saying what you are going to do/order points

In this essay I will … / This essay will … first(ly), second(ly), third(ly) next, then

Adding another similar point

In addition / An additional x is / Another x is

Also / As well as x there is

Moreover / Furthermore / Similarly / What is more

Moving on to a contrasting point

In contrast / By contrast / Conversely

Moving on to a different point

As for / Regarding / With regard to / Moving on to / With respect to

Restating/rephrasing

In other words / That is to say / Put another way / To put it more simply

Introducing alternative views

Alternatively / A different interpretation is / A different viewpoint could be / An opposing view is / Another possibility is / Others argue that / It could also be argued that

Concluding
To conclude, / In conclusion, /
To summarise,

Reasoning:
Cause/result
Because / Since / Therefore / Thus
/So as / This means that /
This results in / As a result /
Consequently / The effect of this is /
This suggests that

Contrasting
But / However / Yet /
On the contrary / In contrast/

Concession
Nevertheless / Despite x it is still /
Although / However

Similarity
Similarly / Likewise / In the same way

Condition
Unless / Provided that / If / As long as

18 Have clear paragraphs

A 2000 word assignment should usually have 7–10 paragraphs. Paragraphs vary in length but as a general rule they should be at least three sentences long; any fewer means you need to develop the idea more, attach it to a related idea or get rid of it. Avoid paragraphs that are longer than half a page – your reader will be getting tired!

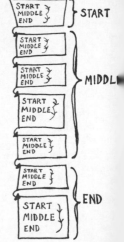

Each paragraph should have a start, middle and end and should focus on one idea. It should have a logical flow and the reader should be able to see (either via a signpost phrase and/or content) how the paragraph follows on from the previous one. At the end of each paragraph your reader should feel that they have read a manageable chunk of your assignment and have reached an appropriate place to pause for thought before reading more.

Below is the third paragraph from the ageism essay (see pp4 and 5). This time I have annotated it to show you the ordering and language techniques you should use to give your paragraphs a clear structure.

Start
Says what
the paragraph
is about.

Middle
Explores the
topic, gives the
evidence and
evaluates it.

Over the last 20 years research has shown that (in addition to) the reporting of conscious negative attitudes towards old people, there also seems to be an unconscious factor involved in ageism. Results from two studies conducted by Perdue and Gurtman in 1990 present evidence for the 'automaticity of ageism', namely that in a memory test, participants remembered more negative traits .. (Importantly,) these traits were not explicitly age-labelled; the participants were making the (negative associations) with older people on an (unconscious or automatic level.) Perdue and Gurtman's findings show that if the perceiver already has encoded negative associations, these can be (unconsciously activated,) (thereby) strengthening conscious negative attitudes and behaviours. In my view there are two minor flaws in the research. (Firstly,) Perdue and Gurtman … the automaticity of stereotyping rather than of ageism. … (Nevertheless,) the evidence of unconscious

Words and phrases

Shows how this paragraph links with the previous one.

Words that highlight key points

Repetition or near-repetition of key words.

Words that show the logical reasoning of the paragraph (E.g. thereby/ also/therefore/ nevertheless/ also)

Have clear paragraphs 81

End
Answers the 'So what?' question - tells the reader why this topic is important in relation to the assignment title.

negative associations with older people is important, not least because (such) associations may go unrecognised and be therefore harder to address and redress, increasing the disabling potential of ageism.

Use of pronouns (E.g. this/these/ they/such) to make links back within a sentence or to the previous sentence.

19 Have a clear style

I have already covered aspects that are essential for giving your writing a clear and appropriate style:

- using facts and logic to argue rigorously rather than giving personal opinion (p22)
- being objective and neutral (p24)
- being specific (p25)
- using source material correctly and precisely (p27–44)
- using appropriate verbs and other phrases to report and evaluate sources (p55–66)
- using *I* and *we* appropriately (p67–70)
- using cautious language (p71–73)
- using content and signposting to give structure (p75–82)

The rest of this section will take you through the other language elements necessary for a clear writing style.

Form and formality

Remember that writing is not just speech written down – students often lose marks because their writing is too much like everyday speech.

Don't
Use contractions – *it's*, *can't*, *won't*.
Use word abbreviations – *dept.*, *govt.*, *e.g.*, *i.e.*
Use vague 'run on' expressions – *etc.*, *and so on*, *and so forth*, e.g. *A healthy lifestyle means eating well, exercising and so forth.*
Use direct questions, e.g. *So, what are the main causes of global warming?* An occasional question for impact is okay but they can make your writing look informal.
Address the reader as 'you' or give them orders (unless giving written instructions), e.g. *You need to think about possible solutions*.
Use rude or emotional adjectives, e.g. *awful*, *ridiculous*, *stupid*, *pretty*, *(very) lovely*, *terrible*, *unfair*.
Use words such as *stuff* or *thing*.
Use words such as a *bit*, *a lot of*, *plenty of*, *huge*
Use the verb *get* or use too many two-part verbs, e.g. *cut down*, *make up*, *got worse*, *brought up*, *set up*, *look into*, *put up with*, *find out*.

Do
Write in full sentences.
Learn how to use punctuation correctly – it is crucial to meaning.
Finish your sentence with as much precision as possible, e.g. *A healthy lifestyle means eating well, exercising, a good work–life balance and a generally healthy environment.*
Use acronyms (e.g. NATO) accurately and give the full form with the acronym in brackets at the first mention.
Use the precise word, e.g. *theory, idea, action, issue, chemical.*
Find precise, formal equivalents for two-part verbs: *reduce, compensate, worsened, raised, established, investigate, tolerate, discover.*

For more advice on good writing style, see Copus J (2009) *Brilliant Writing Tips for Students* in this series.

Don't use speech-like phrases and clichés

These are informal and also often vague and/or meaningless; it's much better to explain exactly what you want to say in your own words.

Don't use …	**Don't use …**
anyway	to name but a few
basically	easier said than done
at the end of the day	that's another story
it all comes down to	to put it mildly
the thing is	keep a lid on
along the way	leave no stone unturned
beyond a shadow of a doubt	a different ball game
in a nutshell	see the light at the end of the tunnel
last but not least	

Power

Academic writing is quite dense and powerful – it packs a lot of information into a small amount of text. Write powerfully by replacing subject/verb phrases and wh-phrases with adjective/noun phrases:

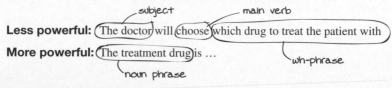

Less powerful: The doctor will choose which drug to treat the patient with
subject   _main verb_   _wh-phrase_

More powerful: The treatment drug is …
noun phrase

Version A below uses lots of subject/verb and wh-phrases. However, the reader does not need to know who is doing what, so the same information can be given in a more powerful way by using adjective/noun phrases (in bold) instead, as in version B.

Version A – less powerful

The doctor will choose which drug to treat the patient with depending on whether he/she has had previous health problems and on what they do for a living. If they are someone who is resistant to penicillin, the doctor will also need to do a skin test so that they can check for reactions that might cause problems.

Version B ✔ – more powerful

The treatment drug depends on the **patient's medical history** and **current occupation**. **Penicillin-resistant patients** will also need a skin test to check for potential negative reactions.

Notice also that in Version A the main points (the treatment drug and penicillin-resistant patients) get a bit lost in the middle of each sentence. In Version B, the use of noun phrases allows the main point to be given at the start of each sentence, which is much clearer for the reader.

Don't overuse abstract nouns

Although it's good to use nouns, don't overuse abstract nouns (nouns that end in *-tion*, *-ism*, *-ness*, *-nce*, *-ity*) as they can sometimes make a sentence clumsy and unclear. It may be better to use a verb/adjective form instead:

✗ *The <u>organisation</u> of the compilation of the legislation was poor.*

✔ *The compilation of the legislation <u>was</u> poorly <u>organised.</u>*

✗ *The <u>significance</u> of the experiment is that it shows that the enzyme is present.*

✔ *The experiment <u>is</u> <u>significant</u> because it shows that the enzyme is present.*

Don't overuse the passive tense

You will sometimes need to use the passive tense but it can make your sentence overly complicated and weak. If this happens, use the active tense instead or leave out the passive phrase altogether.

Passive ✗	Active ✔
It needs to be emphasized that this theory has several flaws. It has been argued in this essay that … It has been recommended by Government that schools require students to …	This theory has several flaws. I have argued in this essay that … The Government has recommended that schools require students …

Strike the right balance of sentence length

It's good to have some short and some longer sentences. What's important is to think about how clear, flowing and powerful your sentences will be to your reader. Avoid sentences that have 30+ words and/or more than two *wh-*, *that-*, *if*, *but*, *-ing* clauses – but also avoid having a whole series of short, bitty sentences.

⊠ One sentence – too long

Online translation programs work via what would seem to be the same process as a human translator, which is to read each word, but the machine does not understand the text content and does not consider the register and context, producing incomprehensible translation that is very difficult to read.

⊠ Five sentences – too bitty

Online translation programs work via what would seem to be the same process as a human translator, which is to read each word. A machine does not understand the text content. It also does not consider the register and context. Because of this it produces incomprehensible translation. This is very difficult to read.

☑ Two sentences – OK

Online translation programs work via what would seem to be the same process as a human translator, which is to read each word. However, a machine does not understand the text content and does not consider the register and context, producing incomprehensible translation that is very difficult to read.

Brevity

Good academic writing is formal but also clear and to the point. Discussing complex ideas does *not* mean that you have to use as many 'long words' as possible, and academic articles that do so are probably poorly written. Aim to convey complex ideas with brevity and avoid using words that are overly complicated:

This essay will *commence with* ✗ / *start with* ✔
The experiment *endeavours to* ✗ / *tries to* ✔
The tower was *fabricated in* ✗ / *built in* ✔
We *utilised* ✗ / *used* ✔ three different methods

or that merely repeat the previous word:

absolutely essential ✗ / essential ✔
past history ✗ / history ✔
conclusive proof ✗ / proof ✔
revert back to ✗ / revert to ✔
hard evidence ✗ / evidence ✔

close proximity ✗ / proximity ✔
different varieties ✗ / varieties ✔
join together ✗ / join ✔
or, alternatively ✗ / alternatively ✔
true facts ✗ / facts ✔

Authenticity

Don't copy someone else's style or use words you don't fully understand; your tutor would much rather see you explain your ideas clearly in less formal words than unclearly in more complicated language. It's useful to remember that if you can't write clearly about something it may be because you don't yet understand it or haven't properly developed your ideas about it. Go back and do some more thinking, planning and drafting.

The main reason for using more formal vocabulary is that it is powerful and precise, enabling you to explain even very complex ideas with brevity and accuracy. It is, however, all too easy to use a word incorrectly or in a 'nearly but not quite right' way.

Examples:

There are a distinct range of ethnic groups in London. (diverse)

Pollution from the new factories has exaggerated the problem. (exacerbated)

Polio vaccinations in the 1960s had virtually prevented the disease by the 1970s. (eliminated/eradicated)

The data infer that lack of sunlight increases risk of depression. (indicate)

The UK population is generally 60,000,000. (roughly)

Remember that it's not enough to know what a word means when you read it – you need to be able to *use* it accurately in your own writing. You need to know:

- The different forms of the word:

    a noun – e.g. *Consideration* of …

    a verb – e.g. We need to *consider* …

    an adjective – e.g. A *considerable* amount of …

    an adverb – e.g. We must conduct *considerably* more research.

- If the word is a noun, whether it is countable or uncountable:

    E.g. You can say *There is one key consideration* or *There are several considerations to take into account*

    but you can't say <u>an</u> important research has been conducted

    or *several important research<u>es</u> have been conducted*

- Common prefixes (such as *inter-*, *intra-*, *super-*, *anti-*, *poly-*, *post-*, *pre-*)

    The negative form of *appropriate* is <u>in</u>appropriate not <u>un</u>appropriate.

- Other words often or always used with the key word (called 'collocation')

    E.g. *Consideration of / under consideration / careful consideration of / to take into consideration*

- Whether the word has a positive or negative meaning (called 'connotation')

    For example you can't say *the increase in pollution has enhanced the problem* because *enhanced* has a positive meaning.

Use words precisely 93

Here are some words common to all academic writing – how many of them would you be able to use with confidence in your own writing?

comprehensive (adj.)	differentiate (v.)	phenomenon (n.)
controversy (n.)	explicit (adj.)	prevalence (n.)
correlation (n.)	factor (n.)	quantitative (adj.)
despite (adv.)	fluctuate (v.)	underlying (adj.)
deviation (n.)	implicit (adj.)	

To improve and expand your word knowledge, develop an active vocabulary learning strategy:

▶ record and *practise using* words that you think are useful or that keep cropping up.

Use a good dictionary[1] (not pocket-size) and if you are not sure which the most useful words are, refer to books and online guides that give common 'academic vocabulary'.

Note that some words (e.g. *solution*) have more than one meaning and are used differently depending on the context or subject. Each discipline will also use some specialised phrases and words, and you will therefore find a subject dictionary helpful.

---

[1] For example, *Longman's Dictionary of Contemporary English*, the *Collins English Dictionary* or an edition of the *Oxford English Dictionary*.

Summary

- It's *your* job to make your assignment clear and interesting for your reader.
- Developing a detailed written plan (set out in paragraphs) will save you time and result in higher marks.
- Structuring your assignment well is not difficult but *is* essential.
- Each paragraph should have its own start, middle and end.
- No amount of signpost phrases or formal vocabulary will make up for poor content.
- Even very complex ideas can be conveyed via simple structure and a direct writing style.
- The key characteristics of a clear writing style are brevity, authenticity, power and precision.
- Only use words and phrases you understand.
- It will take time and effort to develop your vocabulary and style.

Essential element 5:
Rewrite like an expert

21   The process of writing and rewriting

Brilliant assignments are the result of a lot of planning, drafting, rewriting and checking. When you start working on your assignment you probably won't have a clear position on the title (this is a good thing as you should have an open mind not a closed one) and you will also be writing more for yourself than for your reader. By the time you reach the stage of a third draft, however, you should have arrived at an informed position and have a reader-focused piece of work.

Stage in the writing process	Development of your position on the issue	Gradual change in audience from you to your reader
1 Understand the point of your assignment title	Your initial thoughts and views on the main issue.	
(2 Outline plan based on your initial ideas)		Brainstorming, notes on your ideas – **for you**.
3 Reading and research	Development of an informed position through analysis and evaluation of reading.	Notes, summaries and reflections on your reading – **for you**.
4 Detailed plan in paragraphs		Written plan to develop your argument – **for you**.
5 Further reading/research if necessary		
6 Final detailed plan, e.g. 8–10 paragraphs for a 2000 word essay.	Awareness of gaps or faults in your argument. Possible adjustment of position.	Final plan and first drafts in clear paragraphs – **for you and your reader**.
7 First draft. Check against plan and title.	Development of thoughts, ideas and argument and decision on an end position.	

Stage in the writing process	Development of your position on the issue	Gradual change in audience from you to your reader
8 Second draft. Check against plan and title. Add introduction and conclusion if not done earlier. **9** Third draft. Check against plan and title. **10** Finished final assignment.	Full development of thoughts and position that are explicitly and clearly explained in logical stages.	Development of a clearly structured piece of work – **for your reader**. **For your reader**.

Don't worry about grammatical errors in the early stages but do check for them in your final drafts and use feedback from friends, colleagues and tutors to identify mistakes you typically make. You may only be repeating the same few mistakes but these can build up and detract from your work, so it is worth doing a bit of corrective grammar homework in order to resolve them.

Below is a list of the most common errors students make, with the technical grammatical terms given in brackets for your reference.

Sentence grammar

1 Wrong form of the word (adjective, noun, verb, adverb)

Countries are making changes to suit ~~tourisms~~ tourists ✓

There is still a ~~potentially~~ potential ✓ market

2 Incorrect mix of singular and plural for the subject and verb (subject–verb agreement)

The number of tourists ~~have~~ has increased.

Smith et al. (2000) ~~reports~~ report that this level of violence is harmful.

Recent research also ~~show~~ shows that the drugs are effective.

3 Incorrect switches in verb tense (past, present perfect, present, future, conditional tenses)

There are different options for which tense to use – the important thing is to be consistent within each sentence or point.

Wolf (2008) shares this view and Prindle (2009) also ~~suggested~~ / suggests that …

The solution was put into the test tube and ~~has been heated~~ / was heated to …

If this formula were correct, it ~~will mean~~ / would mean that …

4 Sentences that are missing a main verb or clause (fragment sentences)

~~Although there are several advantages.~~

Although there are several advantages, there is also one major drawback.

~~The experiment, which was conducted by a team in London.~~

The experiment, which was conducted by a team in London, will be published next week.

5 Joined sentences that should be separated (run-on/fused sentences)

These decisions can have significant implications, most managers do not receive adequate training. *Replace the comma with either a semi-colon or full stop.*

The web is a constantly developing technology, this can cause data security problems. *Replace the comma with either a semi-colon or full stop.*

6 Wrong choice of *to + verb* or *verb + ing* after the key word (infinitive or gerund)

The model is capable to make / capable of making accurate predictions.

The failure of cells from removing / to remove sugars causes diabetes.

7 Incorrect sentence structure for direct questions

The issue is if / whether this will lead to an increase in violence.

Research was conducted to see what was the cause of the disease / what the cause of the disease was.

8 Wrong word before or after the key word (preposition, collocation)

I will discuss about violence in computer games. (I will discuss violence …)

They are both at / in a constant state of balance.

9 Incorrect use of *the* (definite article)

There are some groups among ~~the~~ society which object to this research.

(… among society ✓)

The study shows that ~~immune system~~ / that the immune system is extremely complex.

(Add *the*)

Punctuation

10 Using commas with *that*

Just about the only time you use a comma with *that* is in the phrase *that is*.

My meeting is on the fourth, that is, Tuesday.

It has been shown in this essay that, ~~this is not the case.~~

It is illogical, ~~that~~ people think pollution is not important.

11 Incorrect use of commas with *which/who* (relative clauses)

If the *which/who* part of your sentence is **essential information** do not use commas:

The experiment <u>which/that was conducted by Smith's team</u> provided useful data.

If the *which/who* part of your sentence is **additional information** do use commas to separate this information from the main clause:

Svennson and Wood, <u>who disagree with Carr,</u> propose a dynamic model of business ethics.

✅ Authors who disagree with Carr are Esty and Collins.

✅ Business ethics, which has become increasingly important, can be defined as principles of behaviour as applied to business organisations.

12 Incorrect use of apostrophes

The apostrophe is never used to indicate a plural and you shouldn't really use short forms (e.g. *do not* > *don't*, *it is* > *it's*) in formal writing, so only use apostrophes to show possession:

The scientific community **of this country** > **this country's** scientific community

The article **of Dr Ashi** > **Dr Ashi's** article

If a proper noun ends with an *s* you can follow the normal rule and write *s's* or drop the second *s*:

The theory **of Dr Jones** > **Dr Jones's theory** or **Dr Jones'** theory

Also note that personal pronouns (*his/hers/its/ours/yours/theirs*) do **not** use an apostrophe:

The title is 'Expression' > **Its title** is 'Expression'

Experts from our universities ✗ / university's ✓ research community developed the drug.

The controversy over global warming stems from the uncertainty of it's ✗ / its ✓ main cause

Other areas to be careful of

- linking words such as *however/nevertheless/whereas* (subordinators and coordinators)
- word forms in a listing sentence e.g. The issues are racism and sexism (parallel structures)
- punctuation
- capital letters
- commonly confused words – e.g. *such as/namely, there/their/they're, affect/effect*.

… so do some homework on these if you have problems with them.

What went wrong here?

This second draft of a paragraph still needs some improvements and corrections in structure, vocabulary and grammar. Corrections are given on the right, but you might like to cover them up and have a go at redrafting the paragraph yourself first.

Draft paragraph

The present financial crisis is a product of world-wide globalization. It can be submitted that the financial crisis results in an increase in the need for litigation, an increase in litigation means financial gain for the law firms. During which the world's have experienced a boom and bust cycle that no doubt will continue to repeat itself.

Comments

World-wide is redundant - globalization is by definition world-wide. Also, the 'topic' sentence has no relevance to the main point of the paragraph, so delete it.

An overly formal and inappropriate phrase for an essay (comes from a phrase used in court)

This is a run-on sentence - needs more than a comma

! Sentence is irrelevant, is a fragment sentence, and uses an empty persuader (*no doubt*).

A review compiled by Anne Lee Gibson, a top American Lawyer who specializes in competition law showed that the top Am Law 100 firms total revenue increased by the greatest percent in each of the three years preceding the appearance of the three recessions since 1984.[6] Recession results of debt, however debt can be valuable when a company goes bankrupt as many have in recent recession, lots of trading debts occurs, this can result in major profit as it is the lawyers who arrange the trading.

Irrelevant information

firms should be firms'

What does 'increased by the greatest percent' mean? percent should be percentage

Run-on sentences - should be split into two or three separate sentences.

Wrong preposition: in not of

Wrong subject-verb agreement. Debts is plural so the verb form should be occur (no s)

You can't just say major profit - should be a significant profit or perhaps large profits

Top tips for rewriting and editing

▸ Read and redraft your work at least three times.
▸ Leave at least an hour between each revision – half a day or overnight is even better.
▸ To help you to see what you have actually written rather than what you think you have written:
  ✔ use printouts for checking drafts rather than checking them on screen
  ✔ read your work aloud
  ✔ get someone else to read it out to you
  ✔ record it yourself and then play it back.

First draft

Ignore language/minor mistakes and check the draft against your plan.

☐ What are your draft's overall strengths and weaknesses?

☐ Does the argument make sense?

☐ Does it answer the assignment title?

☐ Are there any gaps or irrelevancies, e.g. background information, description, digressions

☐ Should anything be in a different order?

You might need to do additional research, fill in gaps, fix flaws in your argument, cut out irrelevant sections, adjust your final position and rewrite whole sections.

Second draft

All of the above + the following:

☐ Do your introduction and conclusion match up?

☐ Does your conclusion *really* answer the assignment title, the full title and only the title?

Check *each* paragraph in the body:

☐ Is the content directly relevant to the assignment title?

☐ Which sentences give the topic, explore it and say what the point of the paragraph is?

☐ Are any paragraphs too long or too short?

☐ Is *your* voice shining through as the dominant one?

Third draft

Read it aloud.

☐ Does the flow/structure need improving or clarifying?

☐ Does each paragraph follow on clearly and logically?

☐ Where do you need to be more brief, authentic, precise and powerful?

☐ Read each sentence aloud – will each one be clear to the reader? Is each sentence grammatically correct as a whole?

☐ Have you given a reference or reminder phrase every time you use a source?

Fourth draft

Where could you still be more brief, authentic, precise and powerful?

☐ Read each sentence aloud again – check again for grammatical, punctuation and spelling errors.

Final check

☐ Check again that you have given some type of reference every time you have used a source.

☐ Check that you have followed the assignment instructions for presentation, reference list/bibliography and any other work (e.g. notes) you are required to submit.

Summary

- Making mistakes and changes is a positive part of the writing process.
- Concentrate on content, general flow and style and don't worry too much about minor grammatical errors until your third draft.
- You will probably get *much* higher marks if you go through your assignment at least three times.
- Learning to read your work with an outsider's eye will enable you to judge the clarity and correctness of your writing.
- Being able to edit your own written work is a valuable career skill, and clear written communication is one of the top five employability attributes.

Final comments

Your tutors give you writing tasks to see whether you have understood the point of the question and whether you have engaged with it at a deep level. Remember that thinking develops writing and writing develops thinking, so don't think of your assignment as separate from studying your subject.

Care about what you write and develop a sense of ownership – it's your name on the cover sheet. Your interpretation of the title, your choice and evaluation of sources and the conclusions you come to are what will make your work unique.

Analyse and take action on the oral and written feedback you get on your work so that your next assignment is even better than your last one. As you progress through your course, think also about how the knowledge and issues you discuss in different assignments connect and relate to each other – not just within one module but also between modules and between levels of study.

You should also gradually develop an awareness of where authors and researchers currently position themselves in your subject – where and how brightly do their stars shine in the disciplinary galaxy? Writing is an important way of identifying where your own star is currently positioned in this galaxy, of joining in the discussion of your discipline and of becoming part of your academic community.

Useful sources

Copus J (2009) *Brilliant writing tips for students*. Basingstoke: Palgrave Macmillan.

Godfrey J (2009) *How to use your reading in your essays*. Basingstoke: Palgrave Macmillan.

Godwin J (2009) *Planning your essay*. Basingstoke: Palgrave Macmillan.

Pears R and Shields G (2010*) Cite them right: the essential guide to referencing and plagiarism* (8th edition). Basingstoke: Palgrave Macmillan.

Williams K (2009) *Getting critical*. Basingstoke: Palgrave Macmillan.

Williams K and Carroll J (2009) *Referencing and understanding plagiarism*. Basingstoke: Palgrave Macmillan.

Index